info

# The Vikings

Stephen White-Thomson

W

Franklin Watts
First published in Great Britain in 2021 by The Watts Publishing Group
Copyright © The Watts Publishing Group, 2021

 Produced for Franklin Watts by
White-Thomson Publishing Ltd
www.wtpub.co.uk

ISBN: 978 1 4451 7365 8 (HB)  978 1 4451 7366 5 (PB)

Credits
Editor: Stephen White-Thomson
Designer: Clare Nicholas
Series Designer: Rocket Design (East Anglia) Ltd
Literacy Consultant: Kate Ruttle

The publisher would like to thank the following for permission to reproduce their pictures:
Alamy: Richard Peel 14(b), Alan King 17(t); Bridgeman: National Geographic 8, De Agostini Picture Library 12(t),
Art and Architecture Collection Ltd 13, Bridgeman 16, 18, © Look and Learn 20; Getty: Werner Forman 5, Hulton
Archive 11(b), Werner Forman 18(b), Hulton Archive 19, Andy Buchanan 21; Shutterstock: Eric Letourneau cover
and 7, Mats O Andersson title page and 17(b), trabantos 6, GTS Productions 10, National Geographic 12(b),
bluecrayola 14(t), ckchiu 15, NERYXCOM 11(t) and 22; Stefan Chabluk: maps 4, 9.

Every attempt has been made to clear copyright. Should there be any
inadvertent omission please apply to the publisher for rectification.

Printed in Dubai

Franklin Watts
An imprint of
Hachette Children's Group
Part of The Watts Publishing Group
Carmelite House
50 Victoria Embankment
London EC4Y 0DZ

An Hachette UK Company
www.hachettechildrens.co.uk

All words in **bold** appear in the glossary on page 23.

# Contents

# Who were the Vikings?

The first Vikings lived in Norway, Sweden and Denmark. From the eighth to the eleventh centuries, they explored many parts of the world. They travelled south-east to Turkey and west to North America.

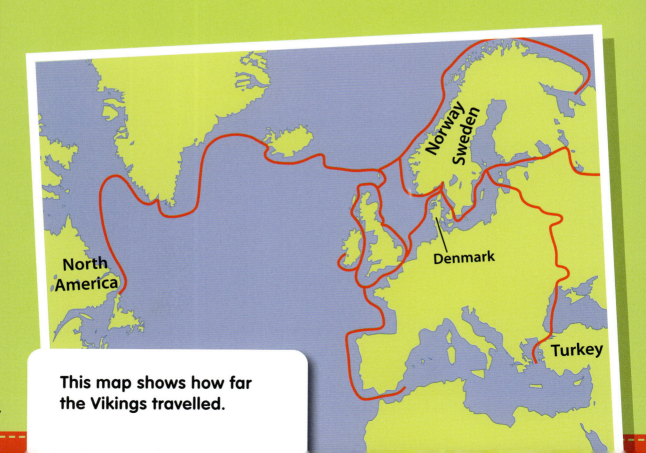

This map shows how far the Vikings travelled.

We know about Vikings because of the objects that **archaeologists** have found. The Vikings were fierce **warriors**. They were also farmers and **traders**, and expert craftworkers.

▲ This beautifully made object was part of a Viking ship.

What do you know already about the Vikings?

# Longships

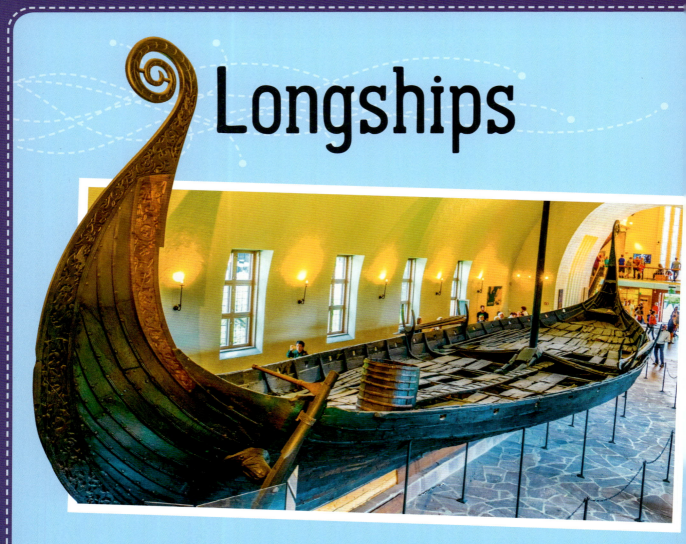

Vikings sailed across seas and up rivers in fast wooden boats called longships. The boats were powered by sails and **oars**. The biggest boats could hold up to 120 people.

▲ This Viking longship had been buried in the earth. It was dug up, cleaned and put in a museum.

Vikings ate fish and bread and drank water on their ships. They slept in sleeping bags made of sealskin to keep them warm and dry at night. They **navigated** by the sun and stars.

▼ This wooden head was at the front of a Viking boat. The Vikings thought that fierce creatures like this would frighten the people they were attacking.

Have you ever been sailing? What was it like?

# The Vikings in Britain

Around CE 790, Vikings began to **raid** the coast of Britain. Most of the people living in Britain at this time were called Anglo-Saxons. The Vikings attacked their villages and **monasteries**, taking **treasure** away with them.

◀ This picture shows Vikings attacking a church.

Land ruled by the Vikings

Land ruled by the Anglo-Saxons

Scotland

Jorvik (York)

**Danelaw**

Wales

England

Have you ever visited York? What did you do there?

In CE 865, a Viking army **invaded** Britain. They fought against Anglo-Saxon soldiers. In CE 878, the Anglo-Saxon King Alfred agreed with the Vikings to divide Britain between them.

▲ The largest part of Britain that the Vikings ruled was called Danelaw. Vikings are sometimes called Danes, because they came from Denmark. Jorvik was the biggest Viking town.

9

# Weapons

Vikings used swords, axes, bows and arrows and spears. Shields were round and made of wood. They had a metal dome, called a boss, in the middle to protect the warrior's hand.

Do you ever dress up and pretend to be someone else? Who?

These men have dressed up in Viking clothes. The swords, spears and shields are similar to the weapons the Vikings would have used. ▼

shield boss

Rich Vikings, called jarls, could pay for metal helmets. Poor Vikings wore hats made of leather. Illustrations sometimes show Vikings wearing helmets with horns on them. But this is probably not true. Horns would get in the way during battle.

▲ This helmet would have been worn by a jarl.

◀ Historians think this stone may show Viking warriors attacking Lindisfarne monastery.

# Houses and homes

Most Vikings lived in villages. Jarls lived in big houses in the centre of the village. They owned land. Poorer people, called karls, lived in small houses and worked for the jarls.

A karl's house

A jarl's house

◀ This is a picture of a Viking farm in North Yorkshire.

This is a **reconstruction** of a Viking longhouse in Shetland, Scotland. ▼

Most karl families lived together in one room. The houses were dark because they didn't have any windows. Karls visited the jarl's longhouse for a feast, or to keep themselves safe if the village was attacked.

This is what we think the inside of a karl's house would have looked like. This reconstruction is in Jorvik (York). ▼

How would you feel if your home had no windows?

# Food and drink

Viking families grew fruit and vegetables, and baked bread. They kept animals, such as sheep, for meat or milk. Vikings collected honey from bees. They made a drink called mead from the honey.

◀ Food was cooked over open fires.

Oats or grain were crushed in between these quern stones. It made flour, which the Vikings turned into bread. ▼

Oats go in here

quern stone

flour

Vikings caught fish from rivers or the sea. They usually ate two meals a day. Some Viking feasts could last for a week!

▼ Vikings dried fish to stop it going bad on long journeys.

How do we keep food fresh today?

# Making objects

Many Vikings were expert craftworkers. They made everyday things, such as combs made out of animal bones. They also made beautiful jewellery. Men and women liked to wear jewellery.

◀ The Vikings wore different types of jewellery.

silver ring

amulet

brooch

gold ring

Do you like to wear jewellery? If so, what kind?

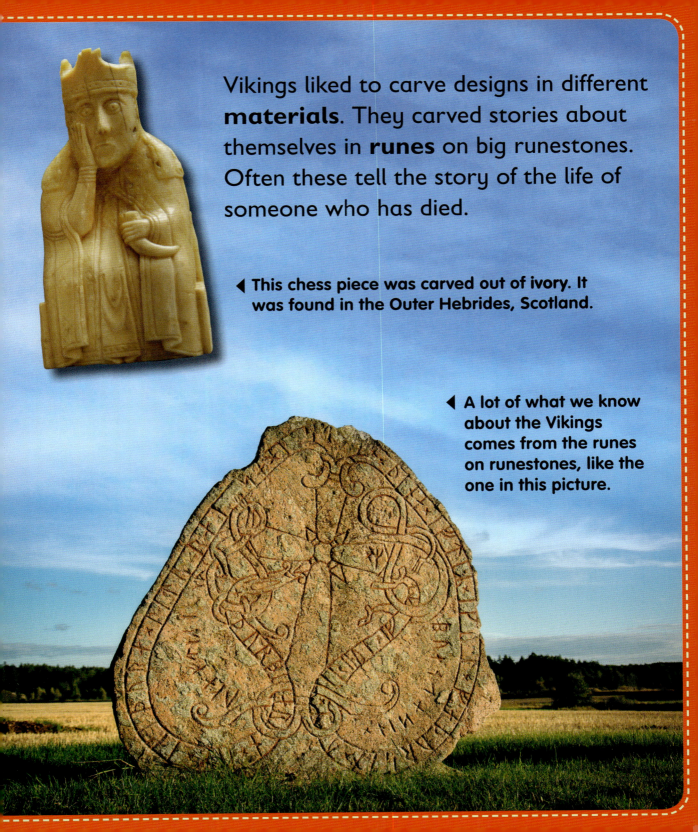

Vikings liked to carve designs in different **materials**. They carved stories about themselves in **runes** on big runestones. Often these tell the story of the life of someone who has died.

◀ This chess piece was carved out of ivory. It was found in the Outer Hebrides, Scotland.

◀ A lot of what we know about the Vikings comes from the runes on runestones, like the one in this picture.

# Gods and beliefs

The Vikings believed in lots of gods and goddesses. Thor was their god of thunder. He made the sound of thunder by banging a giant hammer.

Thor went forth against Jörmungand.

◄ Vikings believed that Thor was strong and brave. They told stories about Thor winning battles against scary animals.

◄ This is an amulet in the shape of the head of Thor's hammer. It was made by a Viking craftworker.

Odin was the chief Viking god. He was the god of war, but also the god of poets. Vikings believed he created the world.

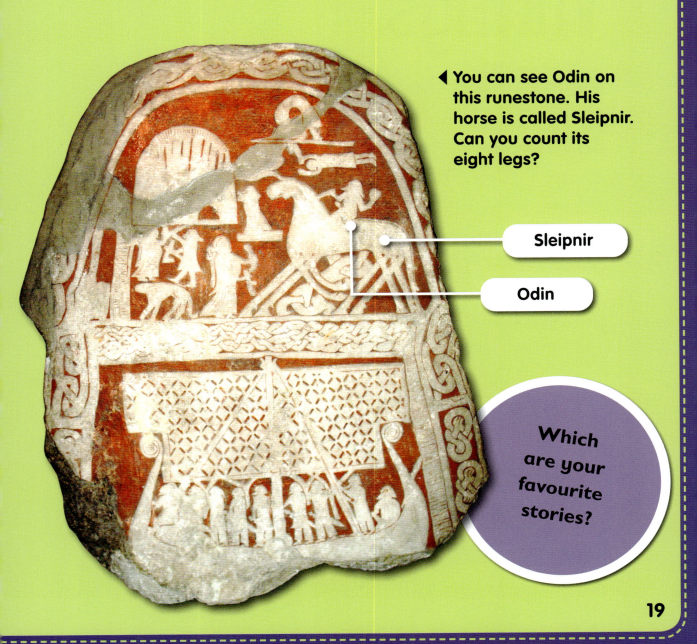

◀ You can see Odin on this runestone. His horse is called Sleipnir. Can you count its eight legs?

Sleipnir

Odin

Which are your favourite stories?

# After the Vikings

King Cnut was the Viking king of England from 1016–1035. The Anglo-Saxons fought against him. By 1042, the Anglo-Saxons controlled England again. Edward the Confessor became king.

▼ There is a story from the time that tells of King Cnut trying to stop the tide from coming in.

When King Edward died in 1066, the Normans invaded from France. Their leader was William the Conqueror. He became King William I (First) of England. Over time, the Viking way of life slowly started to disappear.

Vikings used to burn their famous warriors in longships after they had died. At a festival in Shetland, Scotland, people remember the Vikings by burning a longship. ▼

# Quiz

Test how much you remember.

Check your answers on page 24.

1 Which countries did the Vikings come from?

2 When did the Vikings invade Britain?

3 What was the name of the part of England that the Vikings ruled?

4 Who was the Viking god of thunder?

5 What was the name of the Viking king who tried to stop the tide?

6 Who became King of England in 1042?

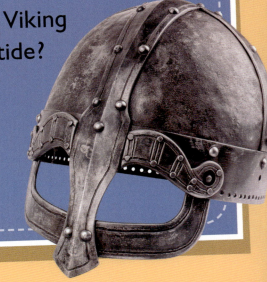

# Glossary

**amulet** – a small object worn to keep the person who wears it safe

**archaeologist** – someone who studies objects left behind by people who lived in the past

**CE** – (common era) refers to dates after CE 1

**invade** – to enter a country and take control of it

**ivory** – a hard, white substance made from, for example, elephant tusks

**materials** – substances that objects are made from

**monasteries** – where monks live and work

**museum** – a building you can visit where special objects are kept

**navigate** – to find your way somewhere

**oar** – a long wooden pole with a flat end that is used to row a boat

**raid** – a surprise attack by a small number of soldiers

**reconstruction** – to re-make something as it used to be, often a long time ago

**rune** – like the letter in an alphabet

**trader** – someone who buys and sells objects as their job

**treasure** – jewellery, money and other precious things

**warrior** – a soldier who is used to fighting in battles

# Index

**Answers:**

1: Norway, Sweden and Denmark; 2: CE 865; 3: The Danelaw; 4: Thor; 5: King Cnut; 6: Edward the Confessor

**Teaching notes:**

Children who are reading Book Band Gold or above should be able to enjoy this book with some independence. Other children will need more support.

Before you share the book:

- What do children know about the Vikings? Did they live anywhere near where you live?
- Show children a world map. Point out the UK, Denmark, Sweden and Norway. Ask children how they think the Vikings travelled to Britain and how they might have travelled around Britain?

While you share the book:

- Help children to read some of the more unfamiliar words.
- Discuss the pictures. Ask children to use the photographs to find out more about Viking clothes, technologies and weapons.
- Talk about why some of the images are photographs and some are pictures. Which of the objects in the images were made in Viking times?

After you have shared the book:

- Talk to your class about Viking place names. Are there places near you whose names end with -by, -thorp or -toft? Were these Viking settlements? Challenge children to find out more about them.
- Work through the free activity sheets at www.hachetteschools.co.uk